The Irish Experience

Katharine O. Engen

D1440261

Contents

Rigby

A Harcourt Achieve Imprint

www.Rigby.com
1-800-531-5015

Chapter One

The Irish Arrive

When most people think about Irish **immigration** to the United States, they think of the mass immigration of the 1840s and 1850s. However, the Irish actually began to settle America in the 1700s, when they were fleeing religious **discrimination** and a lack of jobs. Thousands of Irish arrived each year, hoping for a better life.

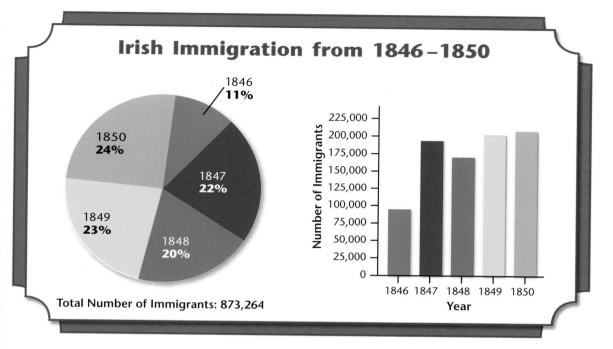

Irish Immigration from 1846–1850

1846 **11%**

1850 **24%**

1847 **22%**

1849 **23%**

1848 **20%**

Total Number of Immigrants: 873,264

Number of Immigrants

225,000
200,000
175,000
150,000
125,000
100,000
75,000
50,000
25,000
0

1846 1847 1848 1849 1850

Year

These early immigrants settled in Boston, Cincinnati, Chicago, San Francisco, and New York City. Most of the immigrants in the late eighteenth century and early nineteenth century were schoolteachers, **craftspeople**, and businessmen. By contrast, most of those who immigrated to the United States during the mid to late nineteenth century were poor farmers and workers.

Life in Ireland was difficult in the 1800s. Most Irish worked on small farms growing potatoes. The Irish depended on potatoes as their main food source because they were easy to farm and very filling. Unfortunately, in 1845 a potato **blight** struck Ireland, turning the potatoes into a soggy, mushy mess. They couldn't be eaten or planted to grow more potatoes. The blight lasted for five years, from 1845–1850.

Irish farmers tried desperately to save their crops. They tried treating the potatoes with a mineral they added to the soil in hopes the potatoes could then be used as flour for bread. They even tried new ways of growing the potatoes. Nothing worked.

This man is working on his potato farm in Ireland. Present-day potato growers don't have to worry about blight as much as their ancestors did.

The results of the blight were devastating. It's estimated that as many as one million people died as a result of starvation and disease during the Irish potato **famine**, or the Great Famine, as it came to be known. About one and one-half million Irish people immigrated to the United States between 1846 and 1855. Many of them settled in New York City.

What Caused the Potato Blight?

Scientists today know that the disease that destroyed the potato crops was caused by fungus. Today farmers use chemicals to help prevent such diseases and keep them from spreading.

These potatoes are suffering from blight.

This family, living in a small, one-room cottage, is trying to survive the Great Famine.

Interview with
Anne McCallister

Anne McCallister's great great grandparents immigrated to the United States from Ireland in the nineteenth century. From their story, we can learn what an immigrant's life was like.

How did your great great grandparents immigrate to the United States?

Anne: Well, they came over from Ireland separately. My great great grandmother, Katie, had her uncle pay her passage. He'd immigrated to the United States during the Great Famine in the 1840s, when the potato crops were failing. He was one of the many Irish people who built the railroads, and he also fought on the side of the North during the Civil War.

Anyway, he knew a family in New York that wanted a **domestic servant**, someone to help clean up and watch the children, and they were willing to hire Katie. So Katie and James—that was my great great grandfather— decided she should go over there first. She saved up enough money for passage for James, and he immigrated to the United States one year later.

Immigrants aboard a ship stare in wonder at the Statue of Liberty.

Chapter Two

A Dangerous Journey

The journey by ship to the United States was the first hopeful step toward a better life, but it was also a dangerous and often tragic step. The ships were unsafe, and since most Irish fleeing the famine had very little money, they were crammed into the **steerage** quarters, or the place where cargo is stored. The more people captains and ship owners could carry on the boat, the more money they made. It was in their best interest to crowd as many people as possible onto the boat.

Passengers traveling in crowded steerage quarters had a difficult and unpleasant journey.

These cramped quarters made it easy for diseases to spread, and this proved fatal for many Irish passengers who were already weakened by starvation. The ships that brought Irish immigrants to the United States were called "coffin ships," since so many passengers did not survive the journey.

Once the ships reached their destination, however, the wait wasn't over. Because so many of the ships' passengers were sick, officials inspected each ship, looking for those whom they felt were too sick to be allowed into New York. These people were sent to the hospital on Staten Island.

After leaving the ship, the Irish and other immigrants were confronted by runners, or people who tried to cheat the new immigrants out of as much money as possible. The runners tried to gain the trust of the immigrants by taking advantage of their lack of knowledge. They would sell immigrants train tickets to other cities at double the tickets' actual prices. The runners would also suggest a cheap place for the new arrival to stay, but the actual rent would be much higher than the immigrant had been told. Immigrants' belongings were often **confiscated**, or taken away from them, at these places when they were unable to pay.

Hundreds of runners would wait at the dock, looking to take advantage of new arrivals.

11

The runners were such a problem that those who had immigrated previously banded together to help pass laws to protect the new arrivals. These laws resulted in Castle Garden, a former fort, which became the entry point to New York, starting in 1855. Here immigrants could be sure of receiving reliable information and help. Castle Garden was the main point of entry to New York until 1892, when it was replaced by Ellis Island.

Castle Garden became a national monument in 1946. Today it is known as Castle Clinton.

Anne McCallister

What was traveling to the United States like for your great great grandparents?

Anne: The voyage over was difficult. They were lucky enough to be able to take a ship powered by steam instead of taking the older sailing ships that previous immigrants had traveled in. The new ships cut the voyage in half, from one month to two weeks. Those two weeks were unpleasant, though, to say the least.

You only got a narrow cot to sleep on, with hardly enough room to turn over. You had to cram your belongings into the tiny space next to your cot, which had barely enough room, even though most of the Irish who were immigrating didn't have many possessions.

Chapter Three

Discrimination Against the Irish

Unfortunately, the Irish faced discrimination in their new lives in the United States. This discrimination was aimed mainly at the poorer Irish immigrants who were hired mainly for difficult and low-paying jobs.

The Irish fought the discrimination against them by becoming a strong influence in politics. They shaped the early Democratic party through their control of Tammany Hall, an organization of politicians that had a lot of influence on laws in New York City.

HELP WANTED
NO IRISH NEED APPLY

BOSTON SIGN CO.

These signs appeared throughout New York City in the 1800s.

Unfortunately, some of the politicians in Tammany Hall were **corrupt**. Although William Tweed, known as Boss Tweed, who was involved with Tammany from the 1850s to the 1870s, provided hundreds of jobs to immigrants, he also stole millions of dollars from New York City. His successor, John Kelly, was able to save Tammany Hall's reputation as an organization that helped the Irish and other immigrants. Tammany continued to help immigrants find work, to aid families with emergencies, and to get laws that would benefit immigrants passed.

In the 1850s, the Know-Nothings, a political movement, tried to prevent Irish from immigrating to the United States. They didn't like the power that the Irish had in politics and were afraid that laws would be passed that favored immigrants over those who had been born in the United States. However, they were not able to halt Irish immigration and quickly fell from power a few years later.

This cartoon and others like it detailing Boss Tweed's crimes contributed to his downfall. Boss Tweed is the character sitting with his leg propped up.

Did your great great grandparents face any sort of discrimination starting out?

Anne: Yes, there was definitely some discrimination. I know that James had a hard time finding a job at first. Some of the employeers didn't want to hire any Irish men. I think that's part of the reason he became so involved with Tammany Hall. He wanted to help other Irish in overcoming discrimination against them. He felt very fortunate to have been able to work his way up, and he wanted to make sure that other Irish had opportunities as well.

This building served as the headquarters for Tammany Hall until 1867, when the political organization moved to a different building.

Chapter Four

Finding Work

Getting a job in New York City in the 1870s was difficult. Many Irish immigrants were unemployed, and when they could find work, their **wages** were low. Many Irish men worked as **laborers** on the docks, in factories, and in construction. The average worker earned around one dollar for a ten-hour work day, or six or seven dollars a week.

The Irish men who were skilled workers or who had some training at a profession were able to earn more money. They worked as bakers, sailors, waiters, and carpenters and could earn up to fifteen dollars a week.

Many Irish men were forced to work long, exhausting hours for little pay.

Dock workers loaded and unloaded cargo.

About forty percent of Irish women worked as domestic servants. They received free room and board, which meant they didn't have to pay rent or for any meals. Domestic servants also earned more than they would at a factory. They were able to save money to bring over family members from Ireland. There were disadvantages to working as a domestic servant, however. Since a woman lived with the family she worked for, an Irish domestic servant had little privacy and had to follow the family's rules.

This Irish domestic servant is caring for her employers' children.

By the 1860s sewing machines were a common tool of seamstresses.

Irish women also worked as seamstresses, dressmakers, and embroiderers, both at home and in factories. Long hours, bad lighting—which was very hard on their eyes—and poor wages made these jobs difficult and demanding. However, the women didn't have to live with a family they worked for, which allowed them more freedom.

Interview with
Anne McCallister

What was that year apart like for your great great grandmother while she was saving up enough money for passage for your great great grandfather?

Anne: It must have been difficult. They were already married, and I know they missed each other terribly. My grandmother has letters her grandparents wrote to each other during that time. Katie felt suffocated by the family she was living with. They wanted her to work sixteen hours a day cleaning, cooking, and taking care of the children. She had to argue with them to get Sundays off, and she felt isolated from other Irish people. James, meanwhile, had moved to Dublin to try to find work. According to his letters, Dublin was very dirty and crowded with people desperate for work. It was not an easy city to live in, and he had to struggle to make enough to survive.

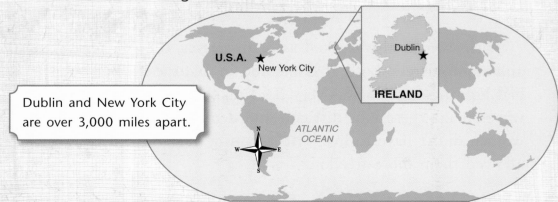

Dublin and New York City are over 3,000 miles apart.

Living Conditions

Tenements were some of the cheapest places to live in New York and the only places most Irish immigrants could afford. Land was very expensive in New York City, so landowners built buildings that could hold as many families as possible in order to make as much money as possible. Tenements were often five or six stories and had very small yards.

Life in the tenements was crowded and noisy.

Tenements were built so close to each other that only the rooms facing the street and the yard had decent light. Most of the tenements didn't have running water, bathrooms, or gas, which was used for heating. Families that rented in a tenement had one to three rooms that were theirs. The rooms were tiny and cramped, but rent was still expensive—around fifteen dollars a month, which was about half a family's monthly income.

Floor Plan of a Tenement

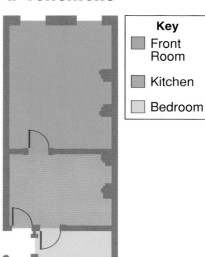

Key

■ Front Room

■ Kitchen

□ Bedroom

Many families not only lived in cramped tenement rooms, but also worked in them.

Interview with
Anne McCallister

How did your great great grandparents start their life together in New York?

<hr>

Anne: They lived in a tenement in Five Points. The neighborhood had been built after the Collect Pond, a nearby lake, was drained because of severe pollution. The city didn't do a very good job draining it, however, and they left a swamp. Those who could afford to packed up and moved to better parts of New York City, leaving the undesirable land for the poorer immigrants.

The Five Points neighborhood no longer exists. Today it is the site of a city park and government buildings.

Anne: Even though Five Points was dangerous and cramped, James and Katie sounded happy there. Other Irish people lived in the neighborhood, along with Italians and African Americans. It must have been pretty lively, with all those different cultures mixing together. Tap dancing was actually invented in the Five Points neighborhood! It was a mixture of Irish dances like the jig and African American dances like the shuffle.

James managed to find fairly steady work as a carpenter, and Katie was doing needlework for extra money. A year later, my great grandfather, Patrick, was born. They moved around a lot, from tenement to tenement, each one a little better than the last.

> Tap dancing was invented in the Five Points neighborhood when Irish immigrants and African Americans shared their traditional dances.

Chapter Six

Life in the Tenements

Irish women usually quit their jobs once they were married. Taking care of their rooms in the tenement was a massive, exhausting job. There were no washing machines, dryers, or vacuums. Most tenements had no running water. The women had to climb up and down flights of stairs many times a day, carrying water up to the kitchen and garbage down to the street.

The women swept the floors with brooms and cleaned heavy rugs by beating the dirt out of them in the yard. They had to go to the market daily, searching for the best deals on food such as fruit and vegetables and on necessary household items, like candles and ammonia for cleaning. They also cared for children.

Laundry was usually done in the street by the water pumps. The clothes would be hung on clotheslines between the tenement buildings. Often dirt and garbage swept out of the rooms above the clotheslines would land on the clean clothes, dirtying them all over again.

Some Irish families took in boarders, who lived with them in their tiny tenement rooms. The boarder paid rent, as well as a small sum to the woman of the house for the extra work she would have to do to take care of the boarder, such as additional laundry and cooking.

Laundry strung out to dry between tenement buildings was a common sight. The clotheslines were also used to send messages to other tenements.

What was life like for your great great grandparents during these years?

Anne: Oh, it was hard. At least, that's what it sounds like to me. My great great grandfather James was working ten-hour days six or seven days a week. Katie had all the housework to do, and she didn't have any running water.

Katie had to carry buckets of water up four flights of stairs! And she had to do it many times a day, for washing the rooms, cooking, and bathing. Can you imagine that? And on top of that, she had to care for my great grandfather, Patrick, and do the needlework that would bring in more money. Both she and James were exhausted all the time. In the next few years, Katie had my two great aunts, Bridget and Margaret.

Interview with
Anne McCallister

What was early life like for your great grandfather and your great aunts?

Anne: I know my great grandfather and my great aunts didn't have a childhood the way I did. They didn't get to play very much. Also, there weren't really many places for them to play. In fact, the first park built in Five Points was Columbus Park, and it wasn't built until 1897, long after they had moved away. They were rarely able to go to school, since the family needed them to help out around the home and to earn money.

It was common to see children roaming the streets, looking for useful items, running errands, and playing games.

Interview with Anne McCallister

Anne: The children helped my great great grandmother with the chores. Patrick helped her bring buckets of water up the stairs, and Margaret and Bridget helped her with the needlework. When the children were old enough, they were sent to the market to buy food. Since the family didn't have a refrigerator, they might have to buy food up to three times a day. The children would also hunt around for wood and coal to use as fuel in the stove.

It was when my great grandfather Patrick was old enough to be hired as a waiter that Katie and James were finally able to move out of a tenement into a **row house** in Brooklyn.

These children are looking for wood, coal, and anything else that might be useful.

Each row house shares common walls with the row houses next to it.

Interview with
Anne McCallister

What was life in Brooklyn like?

Anne: It was much easier than living in the tenement, certainly. They had running water and gas pipes, so the rooms were heated, and they no longer had to carry buckets up and down the stairs. They also had more money now that Patrick was working. Katie could concentrate on the housework, since Margaret and Bridget were bringing in enough money with the needlework they were doing. My great aunts were also able to attend school for the first time. It was the beginning of a better life for my family.

Chapter Seven

The Irish Contribution

The Irish have made many **contributions** to the United States. They helped to build the Erie Canal, railroads, and even the Statue of Liberty. They fought in the American Revolution and the Civil War. In fact, about half of George Washington's army was Irish!

The Irish also made many cultural contributions to the United States, from food to music to literature and art. The Irish also brought St. Patrick's Day to the United States. New York City has been celebrating this festive day with a huge parade since 1756.

Over 30 million Americans—about 15 percent—are Irish or have Irish ancestors. The Irish, as well as many other ethnic groups, still come to the United States, bringing with them their vibrant cultures and varied skills.

Important Events in Irish American History

1846–1855
2.1 million Irish immigrate to the U.S.

1850
Know-Nothing Party tries to stop Irish immigration.

1856
James Buchanan, an Irish immigrant's son, is elected President.

1825

1875

1800

1850

1900

1815–1845
1 million Irish immigrate to the U.S.

1880s
Irish American mayors serve Boston, Chicago, New York, and Kansas City.

38

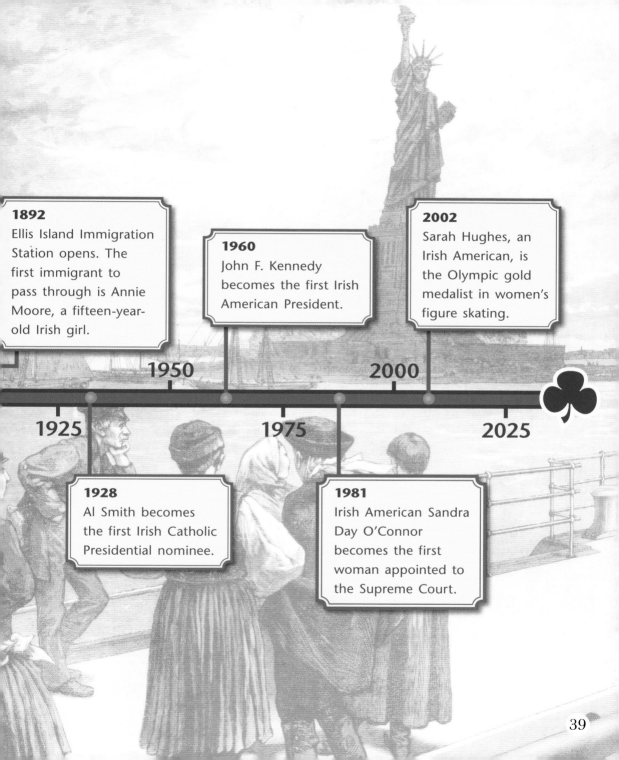

1892
Ellis Island Immigration Station opens. The first immigrant to pass through is Annie Moore, a fifteen-year-old Irish girl.

1960
John F. Kennedy becomes the first Irish American President.

2002
Sarah Hughes, an Irish American, is the Olympic gold medalist in women's figure skating.

1950

2000

1925

1975

2025

1928
Al Smith becomes the first Irish Catholic Presidential nominee.

1981
Irish American Sandra Day O'Connor becomes the first woman appointed to the Supreme Court.

39

Glossary

blight a disease that can kill plants

confiscated taken

contributions important additions

corrupt dishonest

craftspeople skilled workers

discrimination unfair treatment of a person or group of people

domestic servant someone who is paid to clean and cook for a family

famine a long-term lack of food

immigration to move to and settle in a country one was not born in

laborers workers

row house one of many houses connected by shared walls

steerage a section of a passenger ship near the back of the ship where cargo is held

tenements buildings split into many apartments

wages payment for work